HE'LL LOVE ME BY APRIL

he'll love me by april

EMILY NIEBUHR

Emily Niebuhr

Contents

Dedication   vi

FIREFLIES   1

BROKEN JARS   47

FADED WILDFLOWERS   66

BETWEEN THE MOUNTAINS AND THE MOON   90

About The Author   102

for my mom, the firefly in my night

FIREFLIES

you were born with green eyes
and a broken heart
and now you're leaving me in the dark.
am i on your mind this time?
because you're on mine
i'm shivering and shaking
thinking you'll love me for long
we're in it right now
the darkness before dawn.

aren't we really
all alone
in this vast, dark world
little fireflies sprinkling the countryside
threatening to burn it down
warm and waxen
tickling the stars
with our flames
dancing and exhaling
in a haze of our own astonishment.
ours.
this amazement belongs to us
as we wonder what lies
between the dark of the stars
and ponder which wounds
will fade into scars.
darkly beautiful
we chitter and click
a rhapsody of dying embers
glistening and shivering
alone under a tapestry of fire.

lightning bugs
broken bugs
vermillion red scarlet
lonely bugs.

brightly throbbing hearts
beating in unison.

he shivers at the sight
of the torn up sea
blighted, broken
star - pierced ocean

she's dead and gone
cries of pain
long since withdrawn
from the aureate dawn

so he dies
upon looking into her eyes
ghosts of sunrise
whispers in the cobalt waves

sapphire skies
bring him back
to seraphic days.

no stars!
we've made progress.
lights carpet the hillsides
instead of the night.
what a calamity we've created.
we tote our accomplishments proudly,
slamming them into the twin faces
of comedy and tragedy.
how amusing this slow death is!
we cry ourselves to sleep
at the thought of it
while laughing in broad daylight
at everything that melts or burns.
we don't know what court we're playing in
just that we were queens and kings
and now we're jesters.
isn't this funny.
isn't this progress.
how dare you tell us
that we should've kept the stars in the sky.
don't bury this city in shame
it was born of toil and smoldering forest glades
revere that pain.

you couldn't possibly understand
what led up to this point.
it was need
necessity, not greed.
we plucked diamonds and jade
from the earth's heart
so this empire could bear some semblance
to what we all crave

the planet before it became a grave.

she was swallowed by the sky
star-kissed and dancing under moonbeams
to melodies written by the birds

the universe watched every step she took
and covered her path with ruby roses
she tumbled and treaded too close
to those stars
glowing hot and bright

her laughter filled the night
chiming through crisp air
and shocking the world below.

purple lightning bugs
in ceramic jars
that used to be full of honey.
these lonely bugs are lovely
in a way i could never be
they can choose what to see.
for them it's the forest or the sky

staying still or taking flight.

glowing jars line my windowsills
i'll return them once the nightingale trills.
they'll spiral out deep among the wildflowers
under the willow
into her shaded bower.

they blink and burn over brooks and brambles
the loneliest light lands on the blackberry nose
of the newest fawn.
she smells the honey from my jars
and becomes the night sky for one blazing star.

gone with dawn
i break the other stars free
and cut myself on each jagged piece
of the broken jar
i always knew morning would leave scars.

her demise was written by the sunrise,
a story of smoldering stars and seas fated to clash.
blistering flames reflected in her eyes,
turning forests and rivers to ash.

the raven, once a dove,
pearled and snowy before dyed black,
now bears a cross of broken love
with longing scorched upon her back.

we shackled the trembling hand,
that had painted songs across the sky,
forgetting that she brought sunbeams to the land
and broke each day with her euphonious cry.

now fire crests each wave
and birds no longer sing.
locked in glass she watches through her wing
and holds back a cry at
the bloodied hue
of mankind's sky
seeing the tragedy we've made
behind the view.

and so she flies
away from the broken body
this world has made

weary of spiraling
she upturns the fall
and rises to meet the planets

floating on the current
of life's hot glow
and harnessing her embers

so that before she blisters and burns
she can learn
to break the sky.

he was a visionary
rare and fantastically exotic

adventures and oceans seethed
in eyes that held the cosmos

bright patches of lavender and saffron
dappled those hands

colors were etched into his skin
radiating out

threatening to dye
the coming morrows.

we're dancing on the edge of something
with a watermelon wine
spun-sugar sky kind of vibe
and that hard to erase
summer strawberry, sparkling cider
bitterly nostalgic taste.
my bones are lonely
without the song of your heart
pooling in my ears like honey.
this path we're teetering on looks narrow,
studded with wildflowers
and strewn with our marrow.
dark and light, day and night
that's us.
grounded in normality
or pushed into flight
by this rose-tinted reality?
tied together by emerald eyes
and a tether made of stars
and scars not yet carved.
we're dancing
spinning out into the bright,
sun-soaked night.

away from time we ran
my shadow, you, and i
hand in hand
waiting to see
which of us would flicker out
and which of us
would die.

it was you,
it was always you.

clocks
we made them to measure what -
how long it takes
for you to fall out of love
with me?
how long i can last
with all of these memories
from the past
that just won't fade?
how long before
the last tree falls
and the ocean turns black
before time stalls
and nature becomes something
we can't get back?
clocks tick and shiver and sweat
begging me to forget
about the past
and to stretch these moments
into memories that will last,
unlike you and i.
we were always destined
to die.

the girl with purple in her eyes
the one who waits for sunrise
to chirp her song
across the aureate dawn

the shy smile
disguising unspoken trials
the chestnut hair
covering an entire galaxy of freckles
a face of stars, laid bare

the cardinal
the crimson bird
the masked sentinel.

going north, north
to meet her kin.
to see the worth
of what she will be
and what she has been

flying up, up
to kiss the sky
and its flaxen sheen
taking others with her
carrying them on her wings
she sings
she sings
taking flight

slicing the air
with her light.

now he lives
in the washed out violets
and faded vermillion streaks
that the sun watercolors the sky
as it dives
under the horizon

in the lilac soaked air
of an autumn twilight
he dances among
deer and birdsong
in this half-light
in-between time
of shadows and whispers

where her sunlight can't burn
and the starlight
cannot quite
scorch his skin.

it's 2:45
and i wish it was sunrise.
morning promises the day anew
not half spent
through the afternoon.

it's 4:58
in the afternoon
i'm laying under a sky so blue
wishing i never had to move
waiting for the solar system to rise
another blessing for my eyes.

it's 9:34
night has crept through
the crack beneath my door
the constellations march through my window
and watch as I fall
through consciousness and lucidity
through the valleys and peaks of it all
of life and my dreamland
wishing i never had to wake
to reality's bitter hand.

it's winter and summer
autumn and spring
i whirl with the world
attached by a string
to the frost at dawn
and the withering grass

to the people gone wrong
and the time yet to pass.

it's light and it's dark
calls unheeded or harked
unsung and ignored
begged and implored
to be heard and then passed
from my lips to yours.

please know
my walls
have nothing
to do
with keeping
you out

and everything
to do
with keeping
myself in.

why do i try
she asked the sun upon its rise
knowing it would cross the sky
and set on her pain
stealing gold away
replacing bright days
with twilight's orchid blaze.

we exist in pain
spending our lives
pining to dance in the rain
or awaken at first light
to hear the ghosts of aubades
long since withdrawn
by birds that have forgotten their song.

they'll sing
as the sun breaks the sky
imbued not with harmony
but a sorrowful cry.

in pain
in pain
the birds are in pain
they can no longer sing
or fly through the rain

in pain
in pain
the world is writhing and twisting
from wounds we inflict.
the blood won't stop spurting
from tree trunks
and cresting waves
from maroon sunsets
and everything we failed to save.

in pain

in pain
i am in pain.

the ones we can't save
the ones we can't save
i cry for the ones we can't save.

numbered days
for the forest creatures
and bees
and mossy, ancient trees

the ones we can't save.

we try
or we don't
we cry
or we can't.

we care for each creature
from tiger to ant
or we don't

they die
and we cry
for the ones we can't save
the ones we can't save

the shimmering dawns
the cerulean seas
the white freckled fawns
with their star dappled knees.

they match the lights in the sky
in number and brightness
their silence won't lie.

the ones we can't save
our jesters and pawns
the failures, the wrongs
done by us
to the ones we can't save.

sunlight and bright skies
golden zephyrs
and untied times
emerald cloaks
and glass castles
bloodied throats
and ornate tassels.

on paper
they come alive
washed in every color
of the sunrise.

in my mind
they crash and whirl,
imaginary beings
and other worlds.

elven ears
and faerie tears.

i want so badly
what i can't have
so i write down my sorrows
and craft others' paths.

a storybook
a wayward song
an earth shook
a girl gone up in a fiery blaze

writing for those she can't save.

i thought you were my sunrise
painting gold across the skies
at the advent of day
singing melodies with your brush
recklessly spilling color
across the emerging earth
shocking me with
verdant, emerald forests
and crashing, cyan waves

i absorbed the vivid hues
before I realized
to be saved
i needed a sunset
not a fiery muse.

ice dripped down her cheeks
leaving frozen freckles and frosted streaks
steam billowed around her head
in clouds of cobalt vapor
blazing against her hot skin
carving rivers into her fire
sending smoke spirals higher
and higher
waiting and melting and burning
until the smoke
was all that remained
to capture the quiddity
of her rage.

his heart is the image
of an entire cosmos
gone wrong
black stars
a veneer
sheer, but effective
to cloak the inner workings
of a clock so deceptive
that his stars believe
they might not implode
but rather burn, rise, and turn
to join the sun
as it perambulates across the sky
bleeding light into the darkness
within his mind's eye.

you lit me on fire to see how i'd burn
would my flames be cold and indigo like the sea?
would they rip the facade off of me?
would they blind you
with their silver light
or would they flare darker than the night?
i just know
that i'll break dawn
when you use my heart for timber
i'll be the sun's pawn
and scatter the mist
my flames will eat the sky
they'll swallow you too
and silence your cries
you ignited my soul
now you can't put it out
so i'll consume you with ash
and watch as you shiver and shout

can't you pause to tell everyone
that you're really made of
porcelain and fine china

like the dishes
you ate dinner on
at your grandmother's cottage
every Sunday

you could even admit
that your eyes are made of
sunlight sparkling on the ocean
and your ears of birdsong

stop for a moment
tell me about how your mind
is full of words
and your soul
is made of fire.

i always thought you loved me
more than i loved you

but now that you've
broken me

and i'm still glad I didn't shatter you

i realize all along
the opposite was true.

his curse is a mist of yearning
pining for the past with age
longing for the future
after every passing day
grasping only the value of memories
not the moments from which they came
painting bits of childhood
of her
of them
into his mind
brushing color
across the gray portraits of time.

how alone, you are
your emptiness could not be matched
by a foreign star.

blistering beams
torn from the sun
match your tongue
of fire

desire
for your glass
to be shattered
mask ripped away
because we both know
inside that austere castle
of cinders and crystal
no one
would want to stay.

so they noticed her
living in a glass castle with a high-banked moat
taking a walk in the world each day
donning society's jade coat

they wanted to bottle her glow
craving how her spirit split the sky
they watched that blazing bird
unafraid to die
bursting apart
as she flew too close to the sun
so reckless and so high.

he's the type i could break for
i would shatter
and he wouldn't flinch
my pieces would scatter and tremor
and whirl across the sky
and he wouldn't even let out a cry
he wouldn't care if i died
if i woke up and decided
there was nothing left in life to try
i'd tasted every flavor
of ice cream and boy
and known all along
his innocence was a ploy
but i still fell
knowing he wouldn't catch me
i still loved
knowing he wouldn't give it back
my heart or my time
my plans or my rhymes
enveloped by him
the guy who twirls me
around his finger
i bend to his every whim
and now I break.

they taunted him with their freedom
perched on that windowsill
spilling ballads into the dawn air

begging somebody to care
he was
they were
and he could not help
but ache for her

their melodies seeped into his paints
imbuing each hue with forest things
petrichor and faerie rings.

so what if she's made of scorched earth
and she's been to hell and back?
you'd still find a reason to attack
the tears that flow so freely now
the twisting rivers
that fill her soul with diamonds and shivers
because you want to be her
to try on her skin
like another animal's fur
to feel your heart
crackle and splinter
summer frozen over
a girl turned to winter

you two are akin
blood spun into the bodies of twins
you are forest springs
welling with rage
bells' sweet rings
an empty page

but you'll always hate
that she has a reason for her pain
and yours is a broken brain.

you know they're killing you, right?
they're shrouding you with the night
they're stealing your words and your soul
leaving a half dug grave
an empty hole
because your heart throbs too brightly
your bumps and scars make you unsightly
an imperfection in their smoothly shaped reality
an inconsistency that rings of abnormality
a break in the chain
a rattling, shivering queen
who threatens their ability to reign
so they'll kill you
and you'll let them
because they did it so sweetly
the key was thrown away
after they locked you up neatly
and now you're full of poison and gold
heavier than the sum of each star
and all the stories left untold
you've been hushed and smoothed out
smothered and sedated
you've had your last shout
you're a show dog now
a harnessed, slaughter-bound cow
a pawn for progress
a warrior who's been forced to regress
to your battered armor
because the snake
became the snake charmer.

he painted dusk on her
the golden girl
with rain-kissed hair
and sun dappled skin

she sparkled at his touch
and glittered like the sea
knowing his sapphire smile
and her emerald gaze
were meant to be.

fire in her eyes
reflected by each star
frostily they blaze
mind a daze
maze of a soul.

he's under a moon-pierced canvas
gazing at every cosmic thing
taking in their light
realizing that darkness
does not belong to the night
but to the stars in the sky.

you point at the sky
turning my gaze to its lights

almost as though
somehow
you think I'll notice the stars

not the blackness
surrounding them.

BROKEN JARS

if you were equal parts
light and dark
we might've made it
i might've saved it
but i couldn't take it
because you didn't care
your thoughts and feelings
weren't to share
but i craved them
thinking I could bottle them up
and save them
thinking I could send them out to sea
a glass boat dancing on the waves
a watery plea
the words you wouldn't say
the thoughts you wouldn't pray
now i'm left in the wake
of your comet crossed sky
and there's a feeling i can't shake -
all along you wanted someone to hear your cries.

i looked at him
and saw an opal skeleton
with parchment paper skin.
a pleaser, a teaser
a love her, then leave her
dying to capture her as his own
but scared of when her gaze
would dig down past the bone
scared of when his heart's maze
would be unraveled by her own

i saw his brightness
and his fear
and loved it all
forgetting how afraid I was to fall.

he's dying
and nobody can see
that his fire
is turning to ice
or catch the metallic edge
of his bubbly laughter
or notice that the sparks in his eyes
have blinked out
and the sun stopped
beating down on his skin
long ago

the grass is withering and dying
its flowers are shriveling
and collapsing on themselves
just like the universe does
when its stars
can no longer shine
his paints
have long since dried up
with time.

you often find yourself
broken at sunset

as the sky is bloodied
with vermeil rays

and the epiphany
of another spent day
rushes over you

so you hate the nightingale
for the finality in its trill
because you too cannot help but cry
at the passage of time
marked each night by a thousand galaxies
empty of your lover's arms.

because the earth's scars
now outnumber its stars.

because the seas
wear an ebony coat
and the animals
smile with slit throats.

because long before
the last tree withers and dies
you and I will feel
the silence in the skies.

there's a reason
we make wishes
on the comets
that split the cosmos
a reason we marvel from afar
rather than look below our feet and try
to save everything that nature gave.

we look to the night
and its myriad of lights
because we want to take flight
away from the city's ashes
and graying dawns
away from mankind's wrongs.

i say what i need to say
and i do what i need to do
so day by day
people will think they know me
blind to the facade i create
in a crowded room.

and i love who i need to love
and hate who they tell me to
so month by month
i pay
society my dues.

i think the thoughts
i'm taught to think
and i teach the values
i'm told to preach.

year by year
i exist
to live a lie
waiting to die
to escape from a life with
no freedom for my mind.

is it better to exist
under a guise
or to die
loving who they hate
and being barred from heaven's gate

for saying
what i needed
to say?

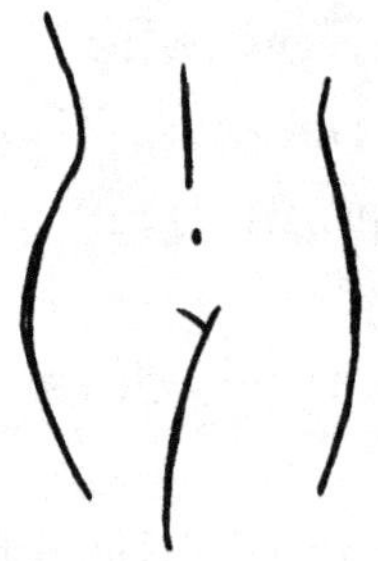

cicatrize my mind
keep my heart behind bars
to escape this time
from the darker scars

the silent ones
the loaded guns
the red herrings
the lack of caring
the empty cries
i can't disguise
or get away from
they breed my need to run
my desire to flee
to race through the air
putting my heart upon a page
pretending that I care
about the people I can't save.

i run,
i cry,
i laugh,
i die.
i break my heart a thousand times
so others won't have the chance to.
i write my pain into these rhymes
so I can keep a bright view.

i sleep,
i rise,
i don my disguise.
i live and cry
then laugh and die.
i break my charade
and chase my dreams
waiting for daybreak,
to enter a life
that's not what it seems.

break each bone
inside my head.
crack my mind's walls
prepare my death bed.

carve the tombstone
pick the flowers
hear the wind moan
as the sky above us showers.

split my heart
with the storm clouds
scatter each part
across the burial mounds.

paint carmine
upon my lips
take out the gun
strapped to my hip.

watch my body
twist and wave
shivering above
my newly dug grave.

cock the gun
narrow your eyes
shroud the sun
steal sunrise.

and sunset,
take them away
break my heart again
and end my days.

if you're emotionally unavailable
and i'm partially unstable
does that put us
where we want to be?

do i want to keep trying
when every day
i feel a little bit more
like dying?

can i afford
to run myself dry
to cut my heart open for you
and bleed into each new sky
knowing the sun will set
on this lie?

i make the plans
i stoke the flame
knowing love is a scam
because your heart won't be tamed.

each day
i kindle the fire
watching the flames flicker
higher and higher

each day
they eat me away
they singe the edges
of my patience
and jade my perception
of romantic relations.

why do people even try
when their partner doesn't bother
to feed the fire
from the other side?

if i could've
plucked the stars from the sky
and spun them into a bouquet for you
i would've,

if i could've painted
every shade of green in your eyes
i would've.

if i could've loved you
with both my heart
and my mind
i would've.

if i had watched the sun
dip below the sea
or pondered the beauty
in the ornate foliage of trees
i would've seen
you and i
are meant to be.

i should've
used my mind
and not wasted my time.

i should've seen
the green in your eyes
was plucked from emerald moss.
you came from the earth,

just like me.
and it's nature and i
that are meant to be.

my identity
was out at sea
hidden away
in the leafy crowns
of aspen trees.

i drowned
in the beauty all around me
and fancied that my eyes
were made of meadows untamed
and my hair of wildfire flames.

my heart was the blackened trunk
of a tree lightning had kissed
a charred stump
a star left unwished.

brooks and streams
sparkled in my eyes
a dazzling display
of water trickling through twilight
when violet mist crawls thickly
in an ethereal fog
the half-light
in-between time
before the storm clouds pass
the eternal night
the shrine
for the starshine
that i used to hold in my eyes

before forest rivers
wrote my demise.

i loved the forest
and the sea
i grew fonder
of the stars
than i should've
knowing i would've become one
if i could've.
i loved the way
the clouds perched above the sky
and how the birds
split the zephyrs
with their drawling cries.

all of this time spent
loving something else
showed me that all along
i had been falling for myself.

FADED
WILDFLOWERS

it was different, how they noticed her
her eyes blazed too brightly
her hands held wild things
she took flight nightly
to rediscover
faerie rings

sunrise was ever present in her soul
and she welcomed sunset
ready to watch the lights
blink out on mankind
prepared to forget
longing to look for beauty
in those lonely stars
suspended above
the city's scars.

i've left too much unsaid.
maybe it's because i'm scared
of what will happen if it leaves my head.
maybe i don't want my jagged lines
on your mind.
maybe i don't want our hearts
to intertwine too closely.
it's dangerous there,
in that land of embers and ash.
where my blood crystallizes and glitters
like the sea after a storm.
i don't want you to follow me
under these slick waves
i don't want you to be torn and tossed
until there's nothing left to save.
let's dance with our backs to the ocean
and look up at the sky instead.
let's listen to the melody
of our electric veins.
let's gaze at the darkly shimmering stars
and let them shed light on our scars.
equal and unsaid
out in the open
finally laid to rest.

compartmentalize
to stabilize
the moving cogs
of my mind.
rationalize
the world through my eyes
to normalize the pain
reality presents
to my heart
and all of its
crooked parts.
apologize
for breaking my disguise
in front of them
when the motions of my pen
weren't enough to conceal
the way my mind bends.
accessorize
my bleeding guise
with baubles and bright things
hoping the sparkles and confetti
will hide how my eyes sting.
immortalize
the nature of this life
suspended in amber
transcending today's strife
search
for silver among the gray
clouded, stormy day
trying to restabilize

my shadowed thoughts
and twilight musings
living in the half-light
of a mind ready to take flight.

she wakes up
to a fever dream
from a life dipped in pretty things
gazing at her star speckled room
looming lights
warding off the night
pulling her deeper into
catatonia and lucid dreaming
shivering below the cold glow
of what she's stumbled upon
after waking from a normal life
strife gone, stunning dawns
all this she soon forgets
upon waking to
her fever dream.

after all is said and done
you'll still be the one
behind the gun
you'll still make the shot
spurring my flight
forever the darkness
inside of this night.
you'll still carve rivers
along my face
you'll still trace quivers
along my spine
suspending me in amber
distorting my sense of time.
i'll still whisper your name
into the dark
searching for the source of my pain
longing for my calls to be harked.
i'll still...
you'll still...
we'll still
chase each other's lies
denying ourselves the thrill
of living untied lives.

it took me a minute
a day
a week
a couple months
to notice
everything that went wrong.
to take off my rose-tinted glasses
and forget about how
you walked me to my classes
and lended me your jacket
and hand
and heart.

but every part
came with a price
you gave me your pain
your joy was my vice
your cracks and scars
locked my mind behind bars.

i cried for the person
you never were
and ached for the love
you gave to her.

i woke with your name
on the tip of my tongue
and replayed your words in my mind
til my heart was numb.

i slept with the dream
of waking as yours
and lived in the grip
of always wanting more.

more time to romanticize
what we could have been
more chances to cicatrize
the promises you carved into my skin.

his emerald eyes wandered
searching for his star girl
and his lips began conversations
with her
-that's what he was used to doing-
until he realized
there was nothing left
to be said

their path in the woods
through the wildflowers
was dead.

he learned
over dusty paint
and cracked brushes
that the people
who are worth
being broken for
are the ones
who will try
to put you back together.

fading canvases
and ephemeral faith

she has a tongue of silver
and a temper of glass.

the sun coated her hair
dazzling surrounding souls
with its golden light
and rarely letting
the hotness of its flame
burn through her veneer.

her glass castle
was melted from the sand
of dying beaches
and forged
in mankind's cold flame

he broke from his reverie
blankly staring
at an empty canvas
trying to stop caring
about the absence of the brush
from his hand
of her hand
from his

tangled and twisted
a garden grows
every time he cries
full of aster buds
and baby-blue-eyes

dappling a verdant carpet
matching the jade
of her gaze
dragging him back
to seraphic, sun-kissed days.

she broke herself
by saving him
and saved herself
by pursuing
every solivagant whim

the winds pulled her
to storm blown seas
and arctic skies
following nature's pleas
and animals' cries

he painted her into every sun
and brook and tree
heart broken, but loving her
for allowing him to see
his unfettered youth
and live as a visionary
even while she split from him
to travel the world
and save the green between the gray.

let the seas rage
and the mountains sing
allow trees to age
and birdsong to ring
rip the metal from the sky
unshroud the stars
free them from their smoky scars
and let the earth cry
in pain
or with joy

let nature belt
its torrential harmony
of felicity draped in calamity
heed its euphonious call
bitter around the edges
like the natural order we've made fall.

let nature be nature again
take the dirt path
plant wildflowers in the grass
and heed fires, earthquakes, and ice
as a warning of our planet's coming wrath.

the brightest smiles
conceal the darkest trials.
white room, spinning
tumbling through space
memories being erased
and evoked
pulled forth, under a spotlight
taking flight
into the fluorescent night
she flees
from her mind
through the halls
racing time
as her life stalls
waiting for her to choose
whether beside the cliff she runs
or off of it
she falls.

this is not vibrant.
this is not beautiful.
this is us
as we roll over continents
and leave ashes in our wake.
this is us
as we divvy up each writhing, bloody beast
and decide what is left to take.
our hands are tied
with ivory chains.
our mouths are gagged
with forgotten names.
and still we dance
on stolen flames.
we carve this world into a shimmering maze
that absorbs every foreign faith
and forest wraith.
this crumbling empire of tangled poison-wood
ate the world
before we caught fire too.
we knew we were on the edge
but we thought this progress would lead us
to the beginning
not the end.

the birch cottage by the brook
the one the forest took
with trumpet vines and lines of ivy
the one the rainstorms shook
but not enough to break
it stands to remind the woods
of what They've yet to take
each mossy stone on the cobbled path
withstanding the sun's wrath
in honor of its past
a shadow life
when the forest was overrun
by parasitic beasts
when They blazed through the trees
and turned woodland creatures into feasts

so it stands
sentry from the past
guarding the golden future
because Their ways didn't last
They were always destined to die.
when the last fish was gone,
the last deer skinned,
and birds no longer greeted dawn,
They realized how They'd sinned
but the cottage stood
when They no longer could
a headstone for the tomb of the woods
slowly being reclaimed
by all that is pure and good.

she dances around my mind
a glass ballerina
in a skirt made from the leaves
on trees during autumn
right before they fall.

she's the director of my thoughts
the one who turns on the projector
in my mind
to entertain me
with memories from summer time.

she paints the walls of my head
brilliant shades of cobalt and red
and carves words across the color
quiescent, hiraeth, aureate
splashing my mind with a picture so ornate
that I can't help but
fall in love
with her.

the dancer, the dreamer
the one we all once were
the child who plucked stars from the sky
and whispered their wishes and plights
into that bright light.

the painter, the poet
the girl with the autumn leaf skirt
the garment that faded

from emerald and jade
to this auburn blaze
of leaves she couldn't save.

she aged with the passage of spring
the departure of summer
the arrival of autumn
and danced through my mind
rewinding time to the memories
of bonfires and waves
picnics and exploring seaside caves.

the projector girl
the director girl
the dancer, the dreamer
the painter, the poet
everything I wanted to be
wrapped into an autumn leaf skirt
now, approaching winter
her leaves will frost over and splinter
the glass girl
will return to her brumal castle
and shut its frigid doors
waiting for more.

BETWEEN THE
MOUNTAINS
AND THE MOON

i know i'll grow old
i'll go gray
then i'll go
i want to know what it's like
between the mountains and the moon

there's stillness up there
winds that shred and scatter clouds
to places farther
than i'll ever go

there are storms of sea and snow
that make monarchs fall
and yellowpines grow

there's a crooked path to reach the top

the place where i can touch the sky
a land of crags and gray
silhouetted against the evanescent day

truth be told
i want to know where i'll be
after i grow old

i've not been so bold as to ask
what choices from my past
have carved the path i'll go
but i do know
my mind has craved
the mountain slopes where wildflowers fade

i've built my glass castle
and my jade throne
upon the bones of beasts we've conquered

when will they learn
that after i go
there will be nothing left to take
the preservation of the world was built on this faith.

truth be told
i've never been so bold as to evangelize
to save people from the world's lies
i'm meant not to judge
my life won't change their lives

my passion grows cold
i search for stories untold
not god

i long for springtime showers
and a thousand yellow flowers
not this facade

i'm breaking and splitting
in the lilac before dawn
it's hard to believe
that adam and eve were when the world went wrong

truth be told
i need to stay here until the mountains fade to gold
i've walked near the valley
and dared to fathom
the possibility of it staying my home

i've watched gnarled mountain paths
melt into purple wildflowers and bronze grass

i've circled the lake and returned to the past
this confusion won't last
won't last

if i stay at the foot of the throne
i'll continue to see birds split the sky and trees grow
but i'm prone to wandering

if i follow this feeling of longing
there's no promise of where i'll go
i've been in the rain and i've been in the snow
these storm clouds won't last
won't last

there are so many questions
that i don't know how to ask

my mind is deep on the bed of the lake
with a god who may or may not be.

a sovereign king who may or may not see
underneath the bright water.

a thousand feet of silver
simmer between the blue and i

my eyes are beginning to blur
i can't quite make out the sky.

breathless and awake
there's an ache under my skin

it threads through my skeleton
and settles in my lungs.

believe also in me
i'm the white sand in the desert
and the leaves on every tree
the scales on the snake
and the ripples on the silver lake
the key to set you free

love my grace
in the face of your broken, tilted heart
it runs in the veins that lace your arms
and soothes your scars

between the dirt and stars
there is ache and hurt
that cuts down past the bone
you'll only lose the pain
at the foot of my throne

until you love me and leave me
you won't be able to find me and see me

i've hidden from the lost
but i know they'll find me
whatever the cost

i'm in the emerald moss
of forest fens
and the crooked brooks
that slip through sun-soaked glens

believe also in me.

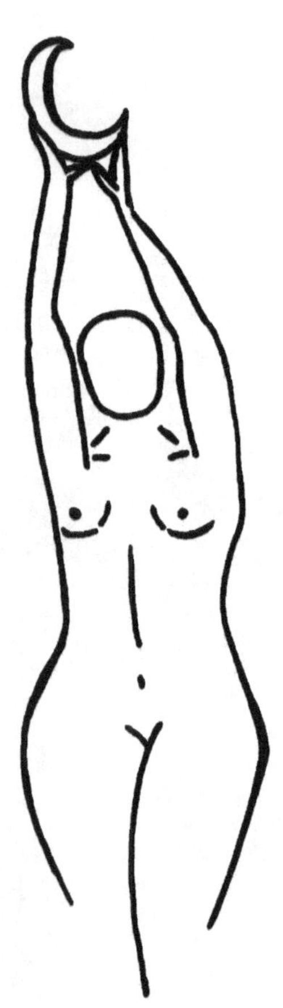

there's no lie in your fire
let me worship your flames
at the foot of this pyre

i think it's lovely of you
to consume me with ash
for a lick of those embers
i'll remember the past

when it was all green, no gray
no cityscapes cracking the blue day
when our seas frothed with fish
and our trees were only half crooked

when the unbroken horse
painted the plains wild
when wing, scale, and sky
constrained our progression
to a manageable lie

and then you broke the veneer of society
you erected skyscrapers from cinders
your civilization persecuted the civilized
it hid under a prim, proper guise

now i sit silently at your throne
as the green shrivels to gray
and think about what i gained from remembering
the last proper day.

a taste of the past in that ash

i saw the furthest stars in your eyes
the ones about to spill over the edge of
the void
swirling and pouring into a place
without comets or nebulas

they sparked and popped brightly
they clawed their way through the dark to me
and brought me back to the edge
of the galaxy

we tipped
and never stopped falling.

About The Author

Emily Niebuhr is a creative writer who resides in San Luis Obispo, California. She loves camping, running, traveling, and anything that involves exploring nature and the world. She believes the earth is sacred and it is our job to protect its remaining wild spaces.